AN ABBEYGATE STREET STORY

STORY

Memories of Abbeygate Street
in the
1920s and '30s

Dudley White

Honey Hill Publishing

Honey Hill Publishing
St Mary's Church, Honey Hill, Bury St Edmunds, Suffolk IP33 1RT

Copyright Dudley White 1999

First published 1999

ISBN 0 9536495 0 4

Acknowledgements: The author would like to thank his nieces Janet Brown and Marion Duncan, and also John Brown and Canon John Hayden and Clive Paine for their help in the preparation of these memories for publication.

Honey Hill Publishing is an enterprise of St Mary's Church, Bury St Edmunds.

Preface

Although I have lived and worked in Bury St Edmunds for over fifty years, I still cannot claim to be a *True Burian.*

I was born in the village of Cockfield, eight miles south of the town, and in the early days of the 1920s the only time little boys came into Bury was during school holidays. We were fortunate to have a LNER railway station at Cockfield, with four trains a day into Bury and the fare about one and sixpence. This was a great treat in those days; otherwise the only way to travel to Bury was by carrier's cart or bicycle and, of course, walking! My father had the village shop, so on Wednesday, which was Market Day in Bury, dad would go into town to do business with various shops. He would take me with him sometimes, not too often! What a treat! This is where I first became one among many others in Abbeygate Street, when the only chance of getting run over was by the errand boy on his bike. Now we have lost the errand boy and his cheerful whistling for ever.

The Abbeygate Street of my recollection is one of private businesses and families 'in residence'. Living over the shop, often in spacious accommodation, was a common occurrence, and many well-known Bury businessmen, prominent in the life and government of the town, together with their families formed a community in the town centre.

I started work in 1925 as a grocer's apprentice with Thomas Ridley & Son at Nos. 35/36 Abbeygate Street. My father had also been a grocer's apprentice; he started work with Mr W. Diaper in the High Street at Lavenham. He later took over the running of Mr Diaper's shop at Parsonage Green in Cockfield and then became the owner of it. We lived behind and over the shop, and from an early age my three elder brothers and I were expected to help out, especially on the many pony and cart delivery rounds to nearby villages. One of our jobs was to help make sausages; two pigs were killed every week to provide pork joints, pork cheese and sausages.

When they left school, my two oldest brothers stayed with my father to help run the business. My other brother, who was very interested in the rapidly growing number of motor cars then appearing in the countryside, went into Bury to become an apprentice motor engineer. When I left school I also came to Bury, cycling the eight miles morning and evening, starting work at 8 a.m. and finishing at 6 p.m. and receiving four shillings a week (20p). My mother equipped me with long white aprons with long ties that fastened round the waist, the top folding over to cover the ties, and the bottom edge was fringed. My first job was in the Tobacco Room. The very first thing I was given to do was to unpack 100,000 Woodbine cigarettes! There were 250 in a box. I also weighed up tobacco and snuff in half-ounce and one-ounce packets. Later on I was put on to making up the tobacco orders for the small shops Ridley's supplied. This was in the days when many goods came to the shop in bulk and had to be weighed up and bagged or parcelled. Sugar, tea, flour and salt, rice, biscuits, spices and many other items all had to be weighed, and treacle, syrup and vinegar came in barrels and were sold loose, having to be decanted into smaller containers. On cold mornings syrup was a slow job; on hot days it was a particularly sticky one. Bacon came in as 'sides' and needed a skilled man to cut it up to ensure the various joints and rashers were obtained economically.

Ridley's was a busy shop, serving families in the town and surrounding villages. It had a high-class trade with many account customers and deliveries to people's homes were regularly made, orders being left or phoned to the shop (in the 1930s and until recently its number was Bury 473). A large order would be sent by motor van, a Delage; smaller orders were taken by errand boys on bicycles. Ridley's had three errand boys then. The residents of Abbeygate Street soon became well-known figures to me and I remember the businesses and the names of the families very clearly.

The Street

If we start from Angel Hill and walk up Abbeygate Street today, the shops and their shop fronts may have changed but many of the upper facades are unaltered and look much the same as I remember them in 1925.

Starting on the right-hand side (at what is now the Scandinavia Coffee House) was Rutter's, estate agents, which until recently was a well-known business name in Bury; next came T.W. Parkington, a military and bespoke tailors, and this family 'lived over the shop'. Mr Parkington was a Mayor of the Borough in 1921. The adjoining shop was Offord's, booksellers and printers, and these premises were later made into two shops, the larger shop being Garrard's the butchers and the smaller Kerry's the florists (Garrard's has become Trotter and Dean and Kerry's is now a wool shop). Next to Offord's and situated on the corner of Lower Baxter Street (now Oddbins) was Bulling's, a medium -class ladies' drapers and outfitters. It was a large shop with a good stock of everything from underwear to hats. The Bulling family lived over the shop and the business continued until well after the Second World War.

Across Baxter Street on the corner (now Abbeygate Lighting) was the premises of Hunter & Oliver, who were wine and spirit merchants. They had a warehouse at the back extending along Lower Baxter Street. A small shop called Burgess, selling pork pies, brawn, sausages and eggs and farm produce in season, such as tomatoes and strawberries, came after Hunter & Oliver, and going on up Abbeygate Street, the next building was the Wine Vaults Public House, previously known as the Gallon Can and now Thresher's. Adjoining this (where Swag Shops is today) was Messrs T. H. Nice, Motor Engineers, with a showroom and petrol pumps at the pavement, hard to imagine in today's largely pedestrianised street. Mr T.H. Nice was also a one time Mayor of Bury. After the car showroom was Collis, the jewellers, then owned by Mr Miles, who lived above the shop with his family.

*This and other advertisements come from
St Mary's Parish Magazine 1927*

The next business was the office of the Bury and Norwich Post, the local paper which later merged with the Bury Free Press. Collis's building and the Bury Post premises (now Coral's) display a Royal Assurance fire plaque which has been renovated in recent years and is now more noticeable.

Still travelling up the street on the right-hand side, the next shop was Hilton's shoes, only recently closed and now a charity shop; then Groom, booksellers, bookbinders and printers, whose printing works was in Hatter Street. The adjoining, particularly tall, building was lived in by the Jarman family, its shop windows displaying photographs of local people and weddings. Mr H. Jarman was responsible for photographing many of Bury's events, buildings and streets and these photos are now of great interest. Mr Jarman was a town councillor and a Mayor of Bury.

This brings us to the former Dunns Bakers and Restaurant on the corner of High Baxter Street where you could meet friends for coffee, lunch and afternoon tea (served by waitresses in black dresses and fancy white aprons) and buy delicious bread and cakes. The business was later bought by Mr R. Willcox, also a councillor and Bury Mayor.

The Champness family lived over the jeweller's shop, which was on the other Baxter Street corner and which is still there with its largely unaltered frontage and landmark clock. The neighbouring shop, again a tall narrow building, was a chemist, Nunn, Hinnel, Clark and Burdon Ltd. Mr Owen Clark was a Mayor of Bury too, and he received the MBE. Long before I started work in Abbeygate Street, (I must have been about ten years old) I remember my father taking me into the shop and Mr Clark showed me the MBE insignia - he also gave me some money; I think it was two shillings.

After the chemist came Oliver's, definitely the top-grade grocer's shop in the town. Its phone number then was No. 1 Bury. It continued in business until the 1960s when it was taken over by Fine Fare and it is now The Baker's Oven, but its frontage looks just the same. There was a shoe shop next called Crofts Shoe Shop (later to become Cash & Co.), and on the Buttermarket corner was Mr W. Plumpton's department store

7

- selling furniture, carpets, household linens, drapery and ladies' clothes. Mr William Plumpton and family lived over the shop premises. The store was enlarged in the 1950s when it took in the Cash & Co. shoe shop premises. At that time it was managed by Mr George Pemberton, another Bury Mayor from 1952 to 1953. The shop is now Palmers. Crossing over the Buttermarket on the next corner (now a travel agency) was the Star Supply grocery store, the manager being a Mr Ford. Then came the steeply gabled building with the niche in the upper part of the frontage. This was T. R. Cross, seedsman and garden supplies. Across Skinner Street was yet another grocer, Walker's Stores. The Corn Exchange completes this side of Abbeygate Street.

Thinking of the shops on the opposite side of Abbeygate Street and going back towards Angel Hill, I start with the Corner Shop selling jewellery, fancy goods and ornaments and run by the Misses Ely. The solicitors Bankes Ashton had the adjoining three storey office and the National Provincial Bank was next door with the manager living on the premises. Then came the red-brick ornamented building occupied by the Alliance Assurance, whose manager again lived above the office; I can remember Mr Willie Ranson and later Mr Linley Berry. Carrying on down the street came Henleys, which sold baby carriages, toys and ladies' and gents' bicycles. This shop had quite a large window display area almost like a small arcade. The Britannia Building Society occupies the site now. This section of Abbeygate Street was completed on the Whiting Street corner by Collen's grocery store, owned by a Mr Whitney and later sold to the International Tea Company.

There has been a chemist shop on the other Whiting Street corner for many years and I can remember at least eight proprietors before the present-day Lloyds. Two of the earlier ones were Scoulding and Cressweller. The Cressweller family lived over the shop and a daughter, Miss Ella Cressweller, married Mr W. Plumpton (from the store across the road). They lived at 31 Crown Street. I remember Day's Shoe Shop next, and it remained, until recently, in the same premises; but Whipps & Co., the fishmongers and game dealers whose open-fronted shop with its large marble slab displaying all kinds of fish and game in season and turkeys hanging all round the shop at Christmas, has gone - its premises have been incorporated into the Midland Bank where, again, in the 1920s the manager lived above the bank. As his neighbour he had the manager of Barclays Bank, a Mr Warne. This bank has also extended its premises since then, taking in the offices of Woolnough, Gross & Chamberlayne, solicitors. Mr Arthur Chamberlayne was the Superintendent Registrar for Bury St Edmunds and his office was where all the local births, marriages and deaths were recorded. He was followed by Miss Kathleen Precious as Registrar. The firm was later known as Gross & Co., and the senior partner, Mr John Knight, was Mayor of Bury on two occasions.

Telephone: Bury 42.

WHIPPS & Co.,

Sole Proprietor: GEO. N. CROGER.

Fishmongers. Poulterers. Game Dealers.

BURY ST. EDMUND'S

AND NEWMARKET.

Best Quality is always the Cheapest.

FAMILIES WAITED UPON DAILY FOR ORDERS.

The next business down the street was again a shoe shop and remains one today. I remember it as Quants. The firm was instrumental in the design of the well-known Startrite Shoes for children. The business was later owned by Mr Mark Petch, who was Mayor of Bury from 1960 to

1961. Yet another Mayor of the borough traded from the next door premises (No. 48) and lived over the shop. This was Mr Aubrey Wilks, Mayor from 1956 to 1957. His was a high-class ladies' outfitters, not a very big shop, but select. The neighbouring shop was a high-class gentlemen's outfitters - the proprietor being Stanley Strickland. Both these shops were where Rumbelows was trading until recently. The premises (No.46) now occupied by Someone Special (children's clothes) and Amanda Jane (beauty studios) was in the 1920s and 1930s a ladies' hairdressers and fancy goods shop run by the Misses Sneesby. On the corner of Abbeygate Street and Hatter Street was Miss Jessie Long's shop which sold sweets and chocolates. Miss Long was aunt to Kathleen Long, the concert pianist. The imposing building on the other Hatter Street corner was the County Club, with its entrance actually in Hatter Street. This building replaced one destroyed by fire in 1882.

Continuing down Abbeygate Street, the next shop (No. 43) was Stead & Simpsons' shoe shop (they had another one on Cornhill) and then came the Prudential Assurance Office. On the first floor here was Mr Alfred Strickland, the dentist. Mr Harold Field and his sisters were the proprietors of the business in the adjoining property (No. 42) with its distinctive curved windows which displayed ladies' dresses, blouses, underwear and hosiery. They also stocked ribbons and buttons and were advertised in the trade directory of the time as 'fancy drapers'. This was another family which lived over the shop.

At No. 40 was a gent's outfitters, then Collinson's and afterwards A.J. Ridley. Here again the family lived over the shop. The exterior of the next premises, Barwell's the butchers, remains much the same; the business was then owned by Mr Ben Lacey, who lived on the first floor with his family, and later run by his son, Mr Maurice Lacey, who was a councillor and a Mayor. A third generation, Mr Christopher Lacey, runs the business today. The shop premises occupied now by Strides (No. 38) was, between the wars, a china and glass shop called Payne's. It stocked china tea services, dinner services, crystal and glassware, ornaments and mirrors. On the Angel Lane corner was Westgate & Sons, corn and seed merchants, who had a mill down in Angel Lane.

The small-paned windows of Thomas Ridley, with the balcony above, are unaltered from when I first went to work there in 1925. However, the curved bow window originally belonged to a separate shop - still Ridley's but this was the Oil and Colour department. In fact there was a narrow door with steps up into the shop right at the centre of the window. The oil and colour men dealt in paraffin and paint and specialised in glass cutting. The first Thomas Ridley lived over the shop and was Mayor of the Borough in 1897. His son, known as Mr Tom, also lived there. From Ridley's to the Angel Hill corner is just a short distance, but there were three businesses. Next to Ridley's (now the restaurant Grills & Gills) was Ronald Bates's radio and radio relay shop where the accumulators for your radios could be recharged. Mr Bates's first wife had part of the shop to sell cigarettes and tobacco and they lived above the shop. Then came Bayliss's tobacco and leather goods shop and the Abbey Cafe run by Miss Jane Smith, whom I would describe as a little 'tea cosy lady', not a bit like a business woman. Finally on this walk up and down Abbeygate Street comes Leeson's the chemist. Sadly, this has recently closed, but when I first remember it, it was run by Mr L.J. Leeson (previously by a Mr Norman) who lived over the shop. What a commanding view of the activities and celebrations on Angel Hill the family must have had.

12

Having completed our walk in the Street, I feel it right to go back to comment on Westgate's seed merchants shop, now Javelin Sportswear. It was a busy place, and of course had its main season in early spring - as the word 'seed' suggests, in February and March it was getting ready for sowing. Some of the cottages in the villages had very large gardens and there were also allotments, where fathers and sons would work to produce extra food for the year ahead. On their half-day on Saturdays they would come into Bury on their bicycles, going straight to Westgate's to buy seed potatoes - Scotch seed, of course. I remember Ernie Walton working late to weigh the potatoes into 7 lb or 14 lb bags and labelling the different varieties. Westgate's had a delivery van which went out to the villages to call on the cottagers - taking seeds for dad's garden, feed for mother's chickens and, very often, feed for the children's rabbits. In the shop itself they always had large open sacks made of hessian, with the tops rolled down to display dried beans, peas, etc. and loose oats and oatmeal. Mothers would go into the shop with their little children, holding one hand tight but not seeing that the other busy hand was putting a little of this into that and a little of that into this! I'm afraid Mr Westgate didn't take too kindly to that. Little dears!

This was Abbeygate Street as I recollect it in the 1920s and 1930s. One or two shops have become offices but several are still in the same line of business, even if the name above the shop is different. Perhaps the main difference is that the community is no longer there - few people live over the shops now. The men who have lived and worked in Abbeygate Street in the past have certainly 'served the town'. I have remembered twelve men who have owned businesses or been connected with businesses in the street who have become Bury's 'first citizen'.

Life at Ridley's

After our walk in Abbeygate Street, I sat and thought about it for a while and it seemed to be an abrupt end to everything: Why end the story there? Whatever happened to the young apprentice after the Tobacco Room? You must remember that at this time I was still only a village boy of 14 to 15 years old. While working one day packing or maybe unpacking, a tall man came to me and said, 'White, from next week you will come through to help us in the warehouse'. I said 'Yes, Sir.' Now I had no idea who he was, only that he wore a long grey coat (the other men wore light brown ones) and no one told *him* what to do! So I asked the young man I was already working with and he told me. This young man was a good friend to me always. The grey-coated man was a director. The firm had four: two in the wholesale department, with grey coats, one in the office accounts department who wore a plain suit, and one in the retail department, another 'grey-coat', whom I had yet to meet. When the day came for me to work over the passage way, it was quite a change. The orders were quite large and goods were in larger quantities. They were in half dozens or dozens, even by the gross; some were in seven pounds, fourteen pounds or hundredweights (112 lbs). Lots of things I'd never seen before. As the days went by I wondered how and where these orders I made up, came from. Well, the two directors made regular journeys on a four-weekly basis out to the villages within a radius of about twenty miles of Bury. They would go off with a case of samples, etc., and the accounts for the last deliveries and call on the village shopkeepers, hoping for fresh orders and cheques to settle the accounts. They were driven by car. Some of these journeys were named after the villages: 'The Rows', because that journey included West Row, Beck Row and Holywell Row. Another was 'The Lophams' and included North and South Lopham. There were also town orders as there were many small general shops then, and they were collected on Mondays by the director in the plain suit. It appeared to be his pleasure and a change from office work.

When the village shop orders were all packed up and invoices ready, the big lorry would load them in the reverse order so that those farthest away would be at the front. This lorry was a Caladon, with solid tyres and chain-driven but, at that time, up-to-date. There was also a smaller lorry, an Austin, with no windscreen and a tarpaulin cover, used for town and station work. This also had solid tyres. Most goods came by rail in those days and there was plenty of station work.

Two of the most outstanding commodities we handled were salt and sugar. Salt came in two stone (28 lbs) blocks. Rock salt was used by farmers to put with horse and cattle troughs for the animals to lick while in stables and barns. This must have been good for them in some way. I must say this salt was as brown and hard as stone and looked like it. Another kind was loose and had to be shovelled from truck to lorry and unloaded at the back of the lorry sheds at what we knew as the salt pit. It was quite a job. I am not sure about this but I think they used wooden shovels because metal ones would have rusted. This was called agricultural or broad salt; of course as time went on it was packed in half-hundredweight sacks. Sometimes it got rather damp. The big houses in those days had gardeners and they had the salt to put on driveways to kill the weeds. In the spring they would also spread it quite thickly on the asparagus beds for the same purpose.

Now sugar. This came in two-hundredweight sacks (224 lbs) and caster sugar came in sacks weighing half that amount, so that was much easier to handle. Loaf or cube sugar came in half-hundredweight (56lbs) boxes. So now you can see the reasons for the bags: blue, quite thick, paper bags which everyone seems to remember when looking back. The customers received their sugar orders neatly packed in 1lb or 2lb blue bags with the tops carefully folded down.

I must mention the sacks the sugar came in. These were quite large and of a fine mesh hessian which did not allow the sugar to sift through. We would often be asked, 'Please when you have an empty sugar sack, may I have it?' Young people today may wonder why. There were two good reasons. The first was that they made very good sack aprons. The housewife would wash the sack on washday, then trim it before cutting it into shape and adding tapes to tie round the waist. The second reason was that the sacks made a strong backing for a 'shred rug'. These were

15

made with small strips of cloth which were threaded closely through the backing with a special tool. The family's well-worn coats, trousers, skirts, etc. would be cut up, and of course the pieces were of many colours, so a nice pattern was often made into the rug. The rugs were thick and strong and lasted for years, usually by the fireside. Today young people would probably say they wouldn't wear a sack apron or have a shred rug, but they ought to remember that, in many cases, it is because of their great grandmother's thrift and good housekeeping that they are where they are today.

In the area of the salt pit I noticed a beam with lots of what I will call pegs, about 8 or 12 inches long, sticking out. They weren't like hat pegs, they were like pieces cut from broom handles, so I thought I must find out what they were used for. I asked one of the older men and he said they were for hanging up the tallow dips to dry out. Tallow dips were like candles and made of mutton fat; a piece of string went through the centre of them and they didn't smell too good! No doubt in former days they were used as cheap candles but I can remember my dad selling them in the village shop at a penny each, mostly in the winter when the snow was on the ground and the tallow was put round the welts of our boots to keep the water out. (No wellies in those days!) All you had to do was to light the string wick and seal the stitches of the welt with the melting tallow. The rack for the tallow dips was a reminder that in earlier days Ridley's were also known as candlemakers.

I was learning all the time, and in what seemed no time, I found I had been working over the passage for eighteen months, and I knew everyone working there by their Christian names, but not, of course, the gentlemen in the grey coats! Oh, it was still 'Yes, Sir' and 'No, Sir'; this was a long time before the modern age when everyone is Tom, Dick or Harry! Just think, prime ministers are, or have been, Maggie or John. I still think familiarity breeds contempt. The men I worked with I liked very much and also the men in the grey coats. Because I was one of the youngest I was teased quite a lot. I remember my dad saying you only tease people you like: those you don't like you leave alone, so maybe they liked me too! Some of their jokes were to send young ones like me on an errand like this: 'Go and ask Ben if we can borrow the treacle sieve' or 'ask Ben for twelve 10-inch chalk lines'; but then came the real test - 'go and ask Ben for six churchwardens'. Now this was a true request because these were long-stemmed clay pipes which came wrapped in straw to stop breakages. I think they sold in the shops for threepence each. The little short-stemmed pipes which the men called 'nose warmers' were a halfpenny. You can see it was not all work; there was always a lighter side to life.

Once a year the firm closed down for a Thursday to give the staff in all departments a whole day's outing. Now we always enjoyed that. Usually it was a visit to a factory with which the firm did business. This may sound dull, but it wasn't! If it was in the London area we would go by train, having breakfast served as we travelled along. I thought this was a real treat! At Liverpool Street we were met by coaches to take us to the factory chosen for the visit. These are some of the firms we went to see: Bryant & May's (we went in with logs and came out with matches!); Lyons tea and coffee and other products; Foster Clark's of Maidstone, Kent, famous for custard powder, etc.; Huntley & Palmer's biscuits at Reading; Cadbury's of Bournville for chocolate and cocoa; Shippam's of Chichester for potted meats, etc., and Van den Burgh in Surrey which produced Blue Band margarine. At all of these factories we would be their guests and they would give us a very good lunch. Then on the way home we would have a really good dinner on the train and a good time was had by all.

Going back to my piece regarding the four directors, of course I knew the gentleman in the plain suit because he was the person my dad did most of his business with, and his family and mine had known each other for many years.

One day while working on orders and anything else I was asked to do, the fourth director, of whom I knew very little, came to me saying that as from Monday I would be working in the retail department (which was the shop in Abbeygate Street), so, 'Ask your mother to get you some aprons ready'. Those were the type I have mentioned earlier - coats and aprons were not provided or laundered.

When the Monday came it was, to use the modern phrase, back to basics. New people to work with, everything in much smaller quantities and many things I had not heard of, let alone seen. As it was a Monday the shop wasn't too busy and it was a day for weighing up various items. I remember standing outside in Angel Lane with another man, using scales on an upturned orange box, weighing up washing soda into quarter-stone blue bags; you see it came in hundredweights. I often think of this now - what if it rained?! Lots of goods came in bulk, such as tea in hundred pound chests; this we weighed out into quarter and half pounds onto sheets of white paper printed with 'Ridley's Special Blend'. Each packet was tied with twine, not just anyhow but into a neat oblong. Coffee was wrapped in the same way but only when required because that had to be freshly ground or sold as beans. When you could wrap a pound of beans on a flat paper properly, we reckoned you had made it! Then you could wrap anything, but I can tell you it took a very long time to master it and to hear 'Yes, that's all right'. Of course many other items were wrapped flat such as currants on a yellow paper, raisins also on yellow paper, while sultanas were on blue paper; this was to brighten up the quality of the fruit. Customers would leave orders to be called for and these had to be packed and tied with string so that they didn't fall to pieces when handed over - this was before the age of 'bung 'em in a box', all that came after the war.

When I think back, many things that are no more come to mind, such as sugar candy on a string and bladders of lard, each weighing 4-5 lbs, which came in wooden barrels. The bladders were pigs' bladders and the lard was sold as 'Farmhouse Homemade' and regarded as better than the imported lard which came in large 28lb blocks. Saltpetre, bay salt and salt prunnella were all used for pickling hams and bacon at home; Day & Martin's blacking in stone bottles was a liquid used mainly for riding boots. (How did you get it out? Well, the Back'us Boy dipped a stick into the bottle, stroked the blackening onto the leather, then polished it up with a piece of cloth until the boots really did shine.) Then there was hearth stone, bath brick, balls of whitening, Sunlight soap (three bars in a square box), household Lifebuoy soap (a piece of this was always at the sink), Preservene soap which was hard and transparent, and John Knights yellow Primrose soap in three-pound bars which were cut into pieces to harden and last longer! Oatmeal bath soap came in large tablets, and a well-known toilet-size soap was Gibbs Noomies, which were sold in boxes of a dozen and were the shape and colour of a lemon and contained lemon juice.

Other items readily available then were invalid goods: Crosse & Blackwell's Calvesfoot jelly in jars; Shippam's beef tea and chicken breasts also in jars; Brand's beef and chicken essence in very small jars, and Valentine's meat extract. All of these were to be had if anyone was really ill. No doubt the parson was praying as well! The shop always stocked a great variety of brushes made by John West's of Braintree. We had hair brooms, yard brooms, bass, dusting feather and cobweb brushes (these last were on six-foot bamboo canes) and scrubbing brushes came as single wing, double wing, double tufted and single tufted. Shoe and nail brushes were also kept.

In the early days the retail department always had three errand boys because at any time parcels had to be delivered to almost any part of the town. Why three? Well, the theory was that two would be out on errands and one would be on standby. Wednesday being Market Day, you can imagine the boys were very much in demand, so they were not allowed a dinner hour to go home for a meal and 'in lieu' they were given a piece of cheese weighing about 4-6 ounces. Not the best variety, of course! No doubt they went down Angel Lane to Berry's the bakers for a penny bread roll to complete the snack. This custom had continued for many years and even after it stopped, the saying which stayed on was 'Have you got your Wednesday cheese?'

One of the most important jobs on Saturday nights was getting ready for Sunday. It meant getting the shutters up from the cellar in proper order and dusting them down. All went well unless some clever person handed them up in the wrong order! Then of course they wouldn't fit or run. After that the shop front had to be washed down, the pavement as well, and this was 8 o'clock in the evening. (By 1946, when I returned to the shop after the War, that ritual had finished and was regarded as a big joke.) Once again I must remind you that the years have passed; it is now the 1930s and I am on the front counter, still doing many of the jobs I have described but also serving customers and displaying goods.

In the late 1930s there was a lighter side to life. We used to have young ladies selling flags on charity days, doing things that daddy would never have allowed, such as chasing us to make a sale. The cost was only 3d, but we didn't have many threepenny bits to spare! Wages were about £2.10s to £3.00 then. One summer's day, in the afternoon there were quite a lot of people out in the street and some were saying 'Here they come', and in a short while we could see the Suffolk Regiment - they had marched from Colchester. We heard they had taken their last rest just out of the town so they could march up Abbeygate Street with backs straight and heads held high, led by the CO on horseback. This was quite a sight to remember.

The big houses were still running with a staff of maids, chauffeurs, cooks and others to help with entertaining. It was at this time when I was serving on the front counter that I waited upon a young lady, and after she had been in several times, I plucked up courage to speak to her. We courted for four years and were married in August 1939, and three weeks later Britain declared war. We had one year of married life before I was called up to serve five years in the Army, two of them in Egypt. In 1946 we had to start our married life again. During the War, Ada, my wife, had been in the Fire Service in Bury. After I was demobbed I was able to return to my job at Ridley's and it seemed that in spite of all that had happened during the War years, things were much the same in the 'Street'. Of course, there were still shortages of many things but as we were British we just accepted it all and carried on.

There were changes however as the years passed: we saw the County Club close and much later the one-way traffic system was introduced. Now you could no longer drive up the street and the sight in days gone by of pony traps, horses and carts, early cars and vans going up Abbeygate Street was just a memory. At least one could still drive down! Now it is even more restricted because we have 'pedestrians only' at certain times and listed days.

20

Another old custom disappeared after the War. This was the placing of black 'mourning boards' over the windows when any notable person died connected with the town, maybe someone in business or a mayor or councillor or a county person. We put the boards in place (much like the shutters I mentioned) with a card on to say who the person was. The three boards may even now be lying discarded in the attic above the shop, gathering dust, and no one perhaps knows that they were once part of Abbeygate Street.

Another thing that has gone is the issuing of Mayor's Relief Tickets. These were given to people who were really deserving cases, maybe because of illness or being out of work or having large families. The tickets (not vouchers) were for food only and had printed on them 'No Tobacco or Alcohol'! Who recommended these families for the tickets I am not quite sure but I had the idea it could have been the clergy in some cases. I used to wait upon a lady every week who was a church visitor for the Cathedral, a Mrs Robertson. One week she asked me if my wife would help her in her church work by visiting people on her list in certain streets on Monday mornings. She was to check if they were well or in need and to collect tuppence (2d) which was recorded on a card called a 'Providence Card'. These had interest added by the church and also a discount on goods given by the trader. They were mainly exchanged for clothes, never for cash, and again certainly not for tobacco and alcohol! When I went home for my lunch the first week my wife did this little duty, she said, 'I have a new title now, it's the "Pence Lady".' Each door she called at, the children shouted out, 'Mum, the Pence Lady is here.'

When I started work in the wholesale department it was situated behind the retail shop in Abbeygate Street. It moved to Lower Baxter Street in about 1928 and the shop was then enlarged. There had not been much room in the little shop, and six to eight customers meant there was hardly any space to move around. The counter was only two yards long, including the flap, so orders were taken standing, with book in hand. Let into this short length of counter was a hexagonal plate of brass; underneath it was another piece like a tray, the same size and shape but with cavities to hold coins. This was the Gold Till. When a gold coin,

21

sovereign or half-sovereign was taken from a customer, it was placed in the rotating tray and moved on one section so the coin was safe and out of sight. The tray gradually filled up and, as it moved round, the first coin eventually dropped into a drawer below. That way, if somebody said they had been given the wrong change, the till could be turned back to see if the customer had handed over a sovereign or half-sovereign to pay for their goods. The till held six coins; not very many were received in a day's trading. Behind the counter was a nest of drawers: the two top drawers held the silver and copper coins in cups made of wooden blocks. This system of keeping the money was before my time. When I started we had National Cash Registers.

Earlier I mentioned the carriers from the villages; on market days they would drive into town, sometimes bringing goods which the village people wanted to sell - chickens, rabbits, eggs, etc. - and notes for the shops for items the village people wanted to buy. It sounds funny today but the country folk didn't come into town very often. The carrier would charge the person for getting the item and the trader would also pay him for the order. The carrier then delivered the item or goods on the return journey to the village in the evening. The carriers always brought orders to Ridley's. Each carrier had his favourite pub, where the ostler would look after the horse and feed and water it. Later on he would harness it for the journey after having received goods and parcels from various shops during the day and making sure they went into the right cart. All parcels had to be sent to these pubs by four o'clock as that was the time the carriers headed for home, some of them having several miles to go. In the dark winter days this was where 'carriage moons' came in. These were the candles which burned in the lights on the sides of the carts and they lasted quite a long time. Some of the favourite carriers' pubs were the Rising Sun in Risbygate Street, the White Lion in Brentgovel Street, the Three Goats with a front entrance in Guildhall Street and a backway and yard in Churchgate Street, the Fox in Eastgate Street, The King's Head on the corner of Brentgovel Street and St John's Street (now Mothercare) and Bird's Stables on Angel Hill which later became Burrell's Garage (where my brother started work straight from school) and is now a cycle shop.

Seasons

Maybe the public never gave it a thought that shops and their owners work on the seasons of the year, as do many other trades, but before I go on to speak about the seasons of the shop year I must say something about the social life of the town, as this brought extra business to the shops.

One of the special occasions of the winter would be the County Ball which was always held in the Athenaeum. This was quite a glittering affair when jewels were brought out from the bank vaults and sometimes well-known dance bands from London came to play. The party would go on until one or two in the morning, when the guests cars would be called. After waiting hours in the cold the chauffeurs were often to be found huddled round the fire in the ostler's room at the Angel Hotel. These happenings would bring extra trade for the Street because the big houses would entertain relatives and friends perhaps for the whole week. For mere mortals like myself to experience what such an occasion would be like, would mean standing outside the Athenaeum to watch the people arrive.

In later years young people have asked who or what is 'county'. That is not easy to explain but the quick answer is 'breeding'. You may become well off, be able to do many things and take part in the social scene, but you are still not 'one of them'. It's just as the saying goes, that you either have it or you don't! The Hunt Ball was another big event much on the same pattern but, dare I say it, with a slightly different guest list.

But to return to the shop seasons. Spring, summer, autumn and winter - we knew them as Christmas, Easter and stocktaking. In October the dried fruits would arrive: currants, sultanas, raisins and the lovely Cape peel, oranges and lemons which had been halved and then steeped in boiling sugar, strained and left to dry with a piece of sugar in the middle. When mother grated the peel for the puddings and mincemeat, it was 'Mum, can I have the sugar from the middle?' The best raisins, called Spanish Valencia, came in boxes of about 12-14 lbs, with the top layer all faced up in a pattern ready to display. They were the most expensive, but before the housewife could use them they had to be stoned, a very tedious job. In later years the Valencia raisins seemed to fade away and Australian ready-stoned fruit took their place. These came in larger cases which had to be broken into smaller quantities and, as with other fruits, cleaned. Cleaned!! You may say you thought they were already clean, but no, as young grocery apprentices we would sit on an upturned box in the back yard with a bucket of cold water and a sieve to let all the stalky bits and dust fall through. The method was to put your hand in the cold water and then rub the fruit round the sieve with the hand not too wet and not too dry - or else! Not a job to volunteer for, but streets ahead of sticky dates on a cold day.

As a senior assistant I used to dress the shop windows towards Christmas time with all the dried fruit, currants, raisins, sultanas, prunes and apricots. They were left in their boxes, which were covered in white decorative paper with a large diamond shape cut out of the middle to show off the fruit and give it a better appearance. This was just an old custom but in those days the housewife used to select her own fruit. As counter assistants, senior or otherwise, we used to greet our customers with an air of interest, complete with book and pencil to record their orders, and we always tried to get them to add items to their lists. Sometimes there were special lines to be offered. These were often quoted by the dozen, half dozen or quarter dozen, and I may say it worked; in fact I remember someone who was known as 'cheaper by the dozen' by one family! After many years of waiting upon the same households and families they became friends too.

Before I go on to the winter season I will tell you about some of these kind people. At the present time there is renewed interest in the Abbey ruins in the Great Churchyard. I remember with pleasure the people who used to live in the houses built into the old walls: Mrs Cauldwell, quite an elderly lady, was one and Mrs Thomas Ferrand, a gemologist, was another; also the Watson family who lived in Sampson's Tower, which is now a Visitor Centre for the Abbey. Ada and I were invited to tea with them one day. Their living room was on the first floor, taking in the whole of the octagonal tower. If you needed to open the large round windows, someone had to lie almost full length to reach the catch because the walls were so thick! There was a very large fireplace with huge logs ready for use. I asked Mrs Watson, 'However do you get the logs up the stairs?' (they had a spiral staircase which was steep). She said they didn't. Apparently one of the boys would lie along the window opening with the other boy outside down below, and they would haul the logs up on a rope! I am not sure how the two daughters helped, but no doubt they had some part to play in the interesting way of living in a home so different from ours. There will be more tea parties to tell of later on, but to return to the shop and the seasonal trade.

It is now early November and Christmas is in sight with all those extra fancy goods arriving! I remember figs, dates and Chinese ginger in very pretty jars, some blue, others with Chinese designs, and often now they can be found in antique shops at quite a price. Then there were glacé fruits from France and Italy, fancy caddies of tea, biscuits in tins of many shapes and interesting decorations, Christmas puddings ready made in basins and also mincemeat in vast quantities. Christmas crackers were always special and very pretty, and some were very expensive but they made lovely table decorations. I always thought I would like to have been a fly on the wall to see the dining rooms of some of the big houses just before someone sounded the gong! Other specialities we sold were Suffolk hams and York hams and good Stilton cheese. I must tell you this story of the days when the local doctors and some dentists with private patients would receive halves of Stilton from grateful patients. In fact on Christmas Eve some of the doctors often had more halves of Stilton than we had left in the shop! We wondered what they did with them all.

As a change from recording memories of the work at that time, I will tell you something on the lighter side because there were such moments. Although this is after the war (1939-45), there was still a day ledger clerk to record any items a customer wished to have charged to his account and to take down any orders from the phone. All this was done by the clerk *standing* at a tall desk, and in the cold winter days Raymond would wear mittens to keep his hands a bit warm; you see, there was no heating and the front door always stood open, winter and summer. Now if you look at the front of Ridley's you will see some steps on the left leading to the private entrance of the flat over the shop where one of our 'grey-coat' directors (H.O.D.) lived. Somehow Raymond always went in this way and made use of the long line of pegs in the hall to hang up his coat. He thought himself a bit of a ladykiller and dressed for the part; he always wore a dark suit and, when going to and fro, his headgear was a light grey Homburg. This would soon get soiled and look a bit weather-beaten, so he would buy a new one and that would mean another peg in the hall permanently occupied because, you see, he just couldn't dump an old friend; so as time went on the row of hats grew. Then one morning when H.H. (a 'grey-coat') came back from breakfast, he came into the shop and with a bit of a glint in his eye he said to Raymond, 'Do you think I ought to put another peg in the hall so I can hang my hat up or will you deal with some of yours.' That was enough and no more was said. It must have hurt Raymond quite a lot to know his hats were going up Abbeygate Street on an open dustcart, but even so there was a bit of style about their journey because the cart would have been drawn by a very large Suffolk Punch. I think the Borough had nine or more of these lovely horses; in the spring and summer, when their work was finished and after they had been groomed, they would be linked together in threes and taken down to the Holywater Meadows in the evening. They were always in a hurry to get there and Mr Bradley had to do a little trot to keep up with them; you see, they knew they were going to lush green grass. But in the morning at about six o'clock it was a different story. We would hear them coming up at a slow plod, plod and Mr Bradley would be saying 'Come on my old beauties'. Well that's what we thought he said!

This next occasion I recall is another invitation to afternoon tea with a customer and family. I will try to tell you about it. Well, one day I was waiting upon this lady when right out of the blue she said 'Mr White, would you and your wife like to have tea with us one day?' This rather took my breath away but of course I said 'Yes, thank you' and arrangements were made. I thought back over the years: I'd had tea with my vicar, lunchtime sherries with a colonel, lunches and Harvest Suppers with farmers, but never tea with an admiral, so this was quite

26

exciting and something to look forward to. Well, the day and hour arrived. I said to Ada, 'They have two cars, a little Anglia and a vintage Rolls Royce; let's hope its the Anglia because if it's the Rolls and the neighbours see us leave in it we will never live it down.' We waited in our front room so as not to keep them waiting but you can guess what happened - yes, it *was* the Rolls and off we went in style but there were no neighbours to see! On our arrival the admiral himself, Vice-Admiral Rivett-Carnac, was waiting at the door. I thought at any moment we would be piped aboard; we had a really warm welcome. I thought to myself, I do hope I can say all the right things. Directly we entered the hall there was a large table laden with carved elephants they had collected on tours of duty. I remarked to the lady how lovely they were and said, 'You have got them all facing the door!' Now in a very loud voice she said 'how clever' many times and 'Mr White, not many people know that'. She said, 'When elephants are in the wild, wherever they are they always want to be somewhere else. So whether you have only one or several, always let them face the door.' After that Ada and I went our separate ways. Ada was shown over the house and I went with the gentleman to his study to see many photographs of places he had been to, and to read lots of reports he had written and kept, thinking they would be nice to look back on when he retired. One photograph was of himself as captain of a battleship, standing behind the three most important people in the world at that time: they were Winston Churchill, Roosevelt and Stalin at the Yalta Conference. After seeing many other things it was teatime, and then we were taken home in the Rolls. It was a most enjoyable afternoon.

This visit had been in the summertime; I must get back to the autumn and winter and all the hustle and bustle of Christmas. The shop was now like a giant cornucopia spilling over with all the lovely things which had been arriving in the months past. I remember all those barrels of white grapes, packed in cork pieces similar to sawdust but leaving some grapes on top for the customer to inspect. If H.H. (in his grey coat) thought a customer was special, he would shout to a junior for a sheet of brown paper to tip some out for her to choose from. Then he would shout for someone to put the rest back again! You see, he had to impress how important the customer was. I think the way we carried on then must have been where television found the name for its programme 'Game for a Laugh'. I remember one gentleman coming in for half a Stilton. The assistant, J.B., brought one half forward for him to taste, using a testing-iron. After smacking his lips the gentleman didn't think it was quite right, so J.B. said 'There's another half here, try this'. The gent smacked his lips again and said 'That's more like it, why didn't you give me that one before?' So it was wrapped up and the gent was quite happy with his choice. Had he been a little earlier the two halves would have been just one Stilton!

Of course there was a lot of hard work and long hours, sometimes to midnight, the nearer we got to December 25th. I think back to all those tasty pork pies which came from Lincoln by train every week. At Christmas there were large ones weighing about four pounds. I know that when we get old we say nothing tastes as good as when we were young, but these were really tip-top, especially the four pound ones. On Christmas Eve H.H. ('grey-coat') would go to J.B. and say 'What have we got left?' and out would come one of these four-pounders. H.H. said with a smile, 'Burrell, you are getting rather good at this, you had better cut it up for the staff'. It had happened before! We had a nice supper that night.

Another line which had to be treated with great care would be trays of Muscatels. If anyone reading this has never seen or tasted them, then I'll tell you about them. They were, and may be still are, available in the high class shops such as Fortnum's in London. They were dried black grapes and came packed in shallow boxes like trays, each one containing about 5lbs in weight, about six bunches to a tray and each bunch tied with a bow of ribbon. Now this is where old people use the phrase 'if only'. You see, when the muscatels were packed, before the lid was put on, a very pretty coloured print of a Spanish lady in full national costume was placed over the grapes. These pictures were usually thrown away when we opened the boxes. Now I think, *if only* I had saved just one.

When I think back, some of the characters who appeared in Abbeygate Street from time to time come to mind. In about 1948 or so there was the man who used to wheel his knife-sharpening contraption down the street to Angel Lane corner to make his stand there. He went to the shops to ask for knives and scissors to sharpen and then he would sit on the machine and treadle away to rotate the sharpening stone. We now see adverts for modern outdoor clothing called the New Wet Look but I think John's hat and jacket must have been the original ones; they were well greased or oiled and had withstood many a shower. He was always a very quiet man and very polite. Another person who came to the street some years before John was a youth with a cart drawn by a well-cared-for donkey. Those of you who can remember the old St Mary's Hospital when it was the Workhouse, complete with Master and Matron, will know that it was also referred to as 'the Spike', where unfortunate people, through no fault of their own, had to spend their last days. Vagrants or tramps could also stay overnight when walking from town to town, and for a night's shelter they had to do some task such as chop wood for kindling and tie it into bundles. These kindling bundles arrived at the shop on the donkey cart and we sold them for three old pence each. Another item we had delivered by horse and cart was the Besom, known to most as the birch broom, for sweeping lawns. These were sold for sixpence (6d) and ninepence (9d) each and they came from the Great Wood, now known as Bradfield Woods at Bradfield St George, and were brought in by a man known as Mr Johnny Cobbold. He made the brooms himself in a shack in the wood itself.

Before I go on to tell about the last of our seasons (stocktaking) I would like to mention what I recall of the outstanding kindness of one of our customers. I think it was in 1948. The then Lord Chancellor of England had his country residence near Bury St Edmunds at Bradfield St George. He was Lord Jowitt, and at weekends when they came to Suffolk I would wait on her ladyship for orders; and a very nice person she was as you will find out as you read on. One day she asked me if I had taken my holiday. I had not at that time, so the next question was 'Would you like to come up to London to visit us in our official residence?' Of course I said 'yes' and the day was arranged.

When I arrived at the entrance to the House of Lords I had to ask the policeman on duty how to get into the private apartments. I showed my invitation card, and no sooner had he seen it than he put two fingers to his mouth and a shrill whistle went out and a man in uniform appeared to look after me. From then onward it was as if my feet never touched the ground; it was an outstanding day. Her ladyship appeared as if from nowhere and we started a tour of the great rooms which seemed to take my breath away; they were really something I will never be able to describe. First we went to the Lords' Chamber to see the area where the Queen sits to deliver her speech at the Opening of Parliament. I also saw the Woolsack. This I hasten to say is no longer padded with wool as its name suggests. I was invited to sit on it! Lady Jowitt said, 'Now that's where my husband sits, complete with wig and gown.' Next we went into the House of Commons, and there I was able to stand at the Dispatch Box where the Prime Minister stands to answer questions. Then we went to Westminster Hall, so large and impressive, and many things were pointed out to me, among them the brass plates on the floor to mark the spot where the kings we remember have lain in state so that people may file past in mourning. As I now sit and remember days gone by, I think of this particular day as a great privilege and of the kindness of Lady Jowitt in inviting me for such a special visit.

Having dealt with the bustle of the Christmas trade, we returned to work thinking 'now it's straight into spring-cleaning and stocktaking', but we soon realised they were not quite the next thing. Why? Because there was that big orange cloud looming ahead - in a word or two, the Seville Orange! From January 1st the housekeeper or cook from the Big House and Madam from the smaller establishment would be asking 'When will the Marmalade Oranges arrive?' It was an annual ritual, something that had to be done - the marmalade making. We had to make sure we had enough preserving sugar in stock. In those days, some 40 to 50 years ago, the ladies would not use any other for marmalade and jam. It looked as if it had been crushed, and when it was stirred in with the fruit it somehow let air in while boiling.

Once the Sevilles had arrived (and the preserving pans washed, along with every jam jar that could be found), they were bought and carried home or delivered; then would begin the 'cutting up' into either thick or thin slices or the 'chopping up', and a right old mess that must have been! In a season we used to sell over forty cases of Sevilles and the greengrocers and stallholders were also busy selling quantities of the bitter fruit. We used to let out on loan a marmalade cutter - like a large mincing machine - you should have seen the state it was in sometimes on its return. Some people washed it really well but others gave it a lick and a promise; so then we had to give it another do before it could be loaned again.

I would think that behind every front door the houses reeked with the smell of boiling Sevilles for quite a number of days! You may say to me 'Did your wife make marmalade and did your house reek of Sevilles?' Oh no! You see, some of the nice ladies used to bring in a sample of their work, so we too had marmalade as it came - thin sliced, thick sliced or chopped. I used to say 'How kind!'

Now I will get back to our last season - stocktaking. This job always took place on the last Thursday in February and every department closed for the whole day. (Usually Thursday was a half-day and we closed at 1p.m.) In the 1920s the first stocktaking days I remember started at 7a.m.; the older men usually started some time before that. Every item in the shop had to be counted or weighed and priced, and all the fixtures dusted and swept out - it was quite a task. It was in fact a huge spring-clean, and when we had finished, the management knew just what was in stock and where it was. The bright side to all this dusting and weighing was going out to the meals provided for us. For breakfast we all went to the Temperance Hotel, which was on the corner of Woolhall Street and Cornhill and owned by the Whitewick family. The Job Centre is now on that corner. After a good plateful of sausage and mash and a large mug of tea we went back to the counting and the dusting. By one o'clock the job was well under way and we would go to another hotel, which could be either the Angel, the Suffolk or Everard's (on the other Woolhall Street corner). This was a much more posh affair.

Eventually stocktaking like this came to an end, and after the war there were new ideas to make the whole operation quicker and there was no closing of any departments. So an important annual event became just a memory of the days when there was more time, plenty of staff, but a lot of hard work!

Earlier in this writing, I mentioned that just after the War we were rather lax in the way we packed and prepared goods for delivery by van, in and around the town. Well, I think I ought to mention that before the time of 'Bung 'em in a box' we had a good supply of wicker baskets to send the groceries out in. These were made by Mr Houghton, who had a retail basket shop a short way down St John's Street on the left, and osier beds in the low damp meadows off Tayfen Road, but of course this area has all been developed.

His baskets were good and strong and lasted a long time. They were oblong and in two sizes; one would fit into the other for stacking and storage. 'Ridley's' was painted on the front of them, but in spite of having the shop's name we lost a few in various ways as they made good log or laundry baskets! It makes me repeat one of H.H's sayings, 'If you leave a loophole they will find it.' Maybe there are still one or two Ridley's baskets around now somewhere.

Someone may say that this next recollection is not Abbeygate Street, but I think it should be included because to me it's rather special. So I will treat it as if it is a favourite book that has slipped from one shelf to a lower one. I am thinking of the chocolate shop called 'Honor Bright' at the bottom of Angel Hill. (The premises are now an estate agent's office.) This business was owned and conducted by a Miss Turney, an expert in her trade. She was a lady one had to get to know to appreciate her kindness and way of business. With all the varieties of beautiful handmade chocolates laid out to choose from, there were no tickets saying 'do not touch'; somehow you knew that would be frowned on as soon as you entered the shop! She remained in business until after the war, but with increasing age and the pace of modern life I expect it all became too much and she retired, but we were to see her about in Bury for some time. I remember one awful wet and windy morning when she came into the shop. She was well equipped for the weather but I said 'Miss Turney, what are you doing out in this weather?' The answer was, 'Well, I'm the errand boy; errand boys have to go out in all weathers, don't they?' So that was that! You see, she was doing a kindness for others who couldn't get out and about. At Christmas time, when she was in business, she would bring me a gift of those delicious handmade peppermint creams, some plain and others chocolate coated. Ada and I were very selfish about these; we kept them for ourselves. Some long time after this and in much better weather, this lady came into the shop and waited to see me. She then handed me a long envelope which had seen quite a bit of service before. I was about to look inside but she said, 'No, not here, but I would like you to have them', and off she went. The envelope contained some very old postcard views of Bury in the early 1900s and before. Some of them are extra long and called Panoramacards, and in spite of their size the postage charged at the time was only a halfpenny. I still have them to treasure as I write this. That was the last I saw of 'Honor Bright', a very pleasant memory.

The author at work

Retirement

Well, the years have passed and I have been employed at Ridley's all my working life. I am much older and I realise that the age of retirement is fast approaching, and I am wondering what I will do after so many years working with so many kind and happy friends and waiting upon people from all walks of life. As many people have experienced before me, it's a fact of life and a true saying that 'the calendar, time and tide wait for no man and are no respecter of persons'. Retirement day arrived and I was to become an OAP and I thought it would pass unremarked: but no, it appeared that there were some people who had other ideas on the matter. Unbeknown to me, three prominent ladies in the town had organised a subscription list to which people I had waited upon for fifty years as man and boy contributed. At a reception one Thursday morning in the Oddfellows Hall in Whiting Street, Mrs Cory, one of the three ladies, presented me with a very nice cheque for quite a large amount and spoke very kindly of me. There were many people there and lots of memories and happenings to talk about. Some of them recalled coming into the shop as children; now they were parents themselves. As I write this it is sad to think that Dr and Mrs Cory, and other customers I remember well, have passed away but I am still able to meet so many people I know when I am out in the town, and it gives me much pleasure to chat about times gone by.

I am now in my mid-eighties and still walk up and down Abbeygate Street, albeit slower than in days gone by. Nearly all the business people I mentioned earlier have died, but to me they are not dead because I can still see them and their loyal employees going about their daily tasks as if it was just yesterday. There would be Mr Wilcox at Dunns Restaurant, holding the door and bowing his customers in for their morning coffee or afternoon tea, with a bow which in these days only royalty get, if they are lucky. I can still see the three directors leaving their motor showrooms with heads nodding and half a pace behind one another as if in seniority. Someone once said, 'Here come the three wise men!'. And at Ridley's window there is Jack Burrell at his bacon slicer. So it goes on, memories and friends, but I feel I should now 'put up the shutters' for the last time on my recollections of working in Abbeygate Street - the mourning boards I will leave to others.

The interior of Ridley's in the 1930s

Postscript

When I wrote the last paragraph, I really thought it was the right time to end these memories. But no! Why? Well, all too soon I was to read in the local paper this news item, 'Historic Shop Faces Closure', and in October 1996 this did happen. Ridley's closed its doors for the last time. To me it was not a shock, but a feeling of sadness after a lifetime working there with so many friends, staff and customers.

The next time I visited Abbeygate Street it was to see the whole of the frontage boarded up, not with the mourning boards, though it would have been an appropriate time to use them. Of course it was a very wise thing to do, to safeguard those lovely windows, which have been there for hundreds of years, from the hands of vandals who would, no doubt, have been delighted to smash them. I am sure the glass in the top row of panes is the original glazing, because when you look through them you get a distorted view. I seem to remember my dad telling me that when he was young a court of law would not accept your evidence if you had witnessed an incident though a glass window, because of the distortion.

I have written an 'Epitaph for Ridleys' (p.38) to conclude this book of memories. Perhaps I can explain a little more about the background to it.

When the mourning boards had been in use they would, later on that day, be carried up to the attic rooms and be left standing tidily in a corner ready for the next time. H.H. ('grey-coat') would make sure this was done. It seems strange, but there was always a certain respect for those three ordinary black boards. Long after I retired I was in the shop one day as a customer when a new man Ridley's had imported came to me saying, 'I believe you used to work here'. My answer was 'Yes, for a little while!' He went on to say 'I've found pictures of three old men in the attic. Can you tell me who they are?' Of course I could tell him, but I was eager to go up to the rooms where, as a boy just starting in the grocery trade, we used to cut wrapping paper and string the paper bags together to hand out in the shop. Of course I was able to tell him who they were! They were photographs of the first three directors when Ridley's became a limited company. They were Mr L .W. Ridley, Mr T. A. Godfrey and Mr H. H. Hubbert. The photos has been taken by Mr H. J. Jarman of 16 Abbeygate Street. I suggested they should be passed to Ridley's Head Office. While I was talking and looking at the pictures, I could see the three black mourning boards scattered about the floor, covered in dust and rubbish, but I didn't comment, although I had thoughts in plenty: Whatever would H.H. ('grey-coat') have said? I don't think I could print that!

So now I will end, and put the shutters and mourning boards up for the last time.

Epitaph for Ridley's, Abbeygate Street, Bury St Edmunds: recollections of a pre-war custom.

At the demise of Ridley's
the mourning boards
like soldiers where they have fallen,
so they lay,
to gather dust and come what may
no one rallied them for this -
their most important day.

The young will ask   -
What did they say?
What did they do?
Nothing I expect.
Oh yes they did, they paid respect.
On that day
they would be washed and dried
and put outside
where the shutters used to go.
Two for the large window
one for the small,
none for the bow.
The little white card would say
for whom they were
washed and dried today.
It would be for someone, their duty done,
had served their Town and County well.

But no one called them for
their final most important day.
Like soldiers where they've fallen, so they lay,
to collect the dust of yet another day.

Dudley White, 24 October 1996

1929/30 An Abbeygate Street Directory

2 -	T. Cross Seedsman & Florist
3 -	Star Tea Co. Ltd
4-9	W. Plumpton & Sons, Drapers
10 -	Crofts Shoe Co. Ltd., Boot Factors
11 -	Oliver, Grocer
12 & 13 -	Nunn Hinnell Clark & Burdon Ltd, Chemists
14 -	Thurlow Champness, Jeweller
15 -	Dunns, Bakers, Confectioners & Restaurant
16 -	H. Jarman, Photographer
17 -	F.T. Groom & Son, Booksellers, Stationers
18 -	S. Hilton & Sons Ltd, Bootmakers
19 -	Bury & Norwich Post
19 -	Mrs Clare Taylor, Corset Maker
20 -	Collis, Watchmaker & Jeweller
21 -	T. H. Nice, Motor Engineer
22-24	Hunter & Oliver Ltd, Wines & Spirits
25-26	Jn Bulling, Draper
27 -	Murdock, Murdock & Co., Pianoforte Manufs
28 -	Wm Garrard, Butcher
28a -	P. R. Kerry, Florist
29 -	T.W. Parkington & Son - Bespoke Tailors
30 -	Rutter Sons & Co., Auctioneers
30a -	Le Roi, Valet Service
31 -	Leeson, Chemist
32 -	Abbey Cafe - Miss J. Smith
33a -	Suffolk Tobacco Co. - Mrs A. Bates
34 -	R. J. Bates & Co., Electrical Engineers
35-36 -	Thomas Ridley & Son Ltd
37 -	Westgate & Sons, Corn Merchants
38 -	A.W. Payne, China & Glass

39 -	Barwell & Co., Butchers
40 -	A. J. Ridley, Men's Outfitters
41 -	J. T. Field, Fancy Drapers
42 -	Alfred Strickland, Dentist
42 -	Prudential Ass. Co. Ltd (Supt. A. E. Cragg)
43 -	Stead & Simpson, Shoes
45 -	Jessie Long, Sweets
46 -	Sneesby, Hairdresser
47 -	Stanley S. Strickland, Outfitter
48 -	Aubrey Wilks, Gents Outfitters
49 -	Quants, Shoes
50 -	Woolnough Gross Son & Chamberlayne, also the Register Office
51 -	Barclays Bank Ltd (Mr Warne, Mgr)
53 -	Midland Bank Ltd (Harold E. Hardy, Mgr)
53 -	Lacey Gooding, Auctioneer & Valuer
54 -	Whipps & Co., Fish & Game
55 -	Chas. J. Day, Boot Maker
56 -	Wm. Stones, Chemist
57 -	International Tea Co., Grocers
58 -	Greene & Greene, Solicitors
59 -	Alliance Assurance, (J.Linley Berry, Mgr)
60 -	National Provincial Bank Ltd, (Percy H. Middleton, Mgr)
61 & 62 -	Bankes Ashton & Co., Solicitors